# CELLOPHANE HOUSE™

Special thanks to Barry Bergdoll and The Museum of Modern Art

# CELLOPHANE HOUSE™

KieranTimberlake

Foreword   Sandy Isenstadt
Afterword   Billie Faircloth

CELLOPHANE HOUSE™
Published by KieranTimberlake, Philadelphia, PA 19130

First printed edition
16 15 14 13 12 11   5 4 3 2 1

ISBN: 978-0-9831301-3-0

Printed by Brilliant Graphics in Exton, Pennsylvania
Bound by Bindery Associates in Lancaster, Pennsylvania
Printed on Burgo Chorus Art Silk Text 100lb (25% post-consumer waste)
and Strathmore Script Smooth Cover 100lb (100% post-consumer waste)
Composed in Whitney Light, designed by Hoefler & Frere-Jones in 2004
and Memphis Light, designed by Dr. Rudolf Wolf in 1929

Book Team:
Alex Cohn, Daniel Cox, Stephen Kieran, James Timberlake, Carin Whitney

Contributors:
Bradley Baer, Roderick Bates, Steven Johns, Elizabeth Kahley, Matthew Krissel, Barry Lehr, Taylor Medlin, Jon Morrison, Jason Niebish, David Riz, John Sellman, Brian Stacy

# FOREWORD

**For many architects** a completed building project is the complex answer to countless questions raised during the course of design. Cellophane House™, however, installed in 2008 at The Museum of Modern Art as part of the exhibition, *Home Delivery: Fabricating the Modern Dwelling*, raises more questions than it answers. The architects, KieranTimberlake, wouldn't have it any other way. In fact, asking questions—about materials and material assemblies during design; about completed projects and post-occupancy patterns after long use—is so central a preoccupation that the firm has dedicated considerable resources to the process, placed it at the core of design practice, and, exceedingly rare among architectural offices, attained certification, which must be audited annually, from the International Organization for Standardization to assure the integrity of its research and design protocols. KieranTimberlake's dedicated research group, a full ten percent of the professional staff, is comprised of individuals trained in fields as disparate as material science, environmental management, and sculpture, as well as in architecture. Together with the architectural team, they ask questions at different scales, almost in different languages, simultaneously. Although a distinct team, the research group is remarkably fluid, coming to a project early, staying for an hour or a month, leaving a project team to deal with a particular issue, or absorbing a designer for another project for a period. To meet some immediate need, designers often initiate research queries that the team then takes up. Such queries may be resolved quickly, or they might become independent projects, pursued for their own intrinsic interest and, perhaps after time, incorporated back into commissioned work.

Cellophane House™ was the beneficiary of several such questions, each arising from different projects and circumstances, coming together to push forward the design, and then disaggregating to infuse and inform other projects. One question, for example, started with some leaky windows. Hired to renovate Berkeley College, a 1934 neo-Gothic dormitory at Yale, KieranTimberlake puzzled over the leaded windows, which enhanced the visual character of the architecture but lavishly dispensed heated air into the New England winter. The architects wondered whether the existing windows, magnificent but inefficient, might, in their permeability, harbor some sort of intelligence, an answer to a question that no one had thought to put to them. The result was not only a commercially viable product, a ventilated, double-glazed window system with excellent thermal performance at a fraction of the lifecycle cost of comparable units. It also maintained the leaded panes that contribute so substantially to the personality of the Yale campus.

Consistent with the firm's research proclivities, the window's cavity took on its own life as a research query: How to make enclosures perform in relation to manifold constraints at ever finer levels of specificity—that is, how to make enclosures do more. An exterior wall's thermal mass, for example, has long been recognized as an important design factor, right alongside its ability to bear weight. But as thin-walled, frame construction became common for large buildings in the 20th century, architects sought to reconceive enclosure in relation to additional functions. One idea was to consider the exterior as a filter, capable of selectively facilitating or impeding various flows between inside and out, whether light or heat or sound. The idea was spurred by developments in the glass industry, which had learned how to laminate films to filter, say, ultraviolet light for use on camera lenses. Glass was becoming smarter: by virtue of its composite material properties it could select which radiant phenomena it would allow to pass and which it would block. As a 1948 article in *Architectural Forum* put it, the wall "has become a filter between exterior and interior environment rather than a simple barrier."[1] Coincidentally,

---

[1] *Architectural Forum* v. 89 (Nov. 1948): 134-41.

perhaps, selective transparency was at that moment the primary selling point of the house's namesake. As a 1948 DuPont advertisement had it: "Cellophane shows what it protects!...Protects what it shows!" In other words, cellophane was transparent to visible light but opaque to water vapor, a capacity DuPont researchers had focused on in an effort to improve earlier patents.

In 2003, KieranTimberlake contributed further to this longstanding investigation with SmartWrap™, a composite of materials that asked whether enclosure might also be power plant and dispersed communications center, as well as filter. In designing Cellophane House™, the architects turned to SmartWrap™ and asked, reasonably if predictably, just how efficiently polymer film, when used to make an enclosure, would transmit light. But they also asked, unexpectedly, how well it stiffened in an internal frame. Improbably, they pressed on to ask how, exactly, impressions of a passing phenomenon, such as sunlight, might imprint itself on such a material, anticipating that the enclosure might become the primary source of energy. And by this point rather relentlessly, they asked how it would be drawn and formed, laminated, bent and cut, packed and transported, assembled and disassembled, stored and, eventually, re-used. How much energy would it take in its manufacture, use, and re-use, and how would that sum compare to other materials that might serve similar needs? The result was an integrated building skin comprised of multiple layers, each delegated specific tasks of addressing weather, harvesting light for electricity or signals, insulating the interior and channeling warmed air into or away from habitable spaces, mediating solar heat and ultraviolet light, and, finally, serving as an easily maintained interior finish.

When SmartWrap™ was introduced, as the first in a series of exhibitions held at the Cooper-Hewitt, National Design Museum on advanced design innovations, it was supported by an off-the-shelf metal frame selected as much for convenience as anything else. But the design team at Kieran-Timberlake recognized intense research when they saw it, in this case a highly-engineered extruded aluminum modular strut system manufactured by Bosch Rexroth and used for the variable loads and precise tolerances of industrial applications. The design of a retreat home for Stephen Kieran's family was turned into a research project to test the theories put forth in Kieran and Timberlake's 2004 book *refabricating Architecture*. It was also an opportunity to articulate a new question: What more can the framing system do? Completed in 2006, Loblolly House, named for the trees it stands among, is a two-story enclosure framed with the Bosch Rexroth system and adapted for dynamic weather and wind conditions rather than the static climate of a factory interior. At Loblolly House, the integral grooves along the edges of the extrusions, by substituting a dry friction connection for the usual alternatives of nails, screws, glues, and welds, facilitated rapid assembly both of structural components and off-site fabricated elements, allowed great flexibility in locating partitions, and will enable disassembly, rather than demolition, at the end of the building's life cycle.

Although successfully supporting a finished home, the framing system was interrogated further: How high might it go? Would it work for a vertically oriented house, such as Cellophane House™ would have to be, located among high-rises in midtown Manhattan? As the framing system, window cavity, and SmartWrap™, along with a number of other architectural ideas, converged in the design of Cellophane House™, such questions were put to every element, and every assembly of elements, so that at MoMA stood a project that exemplified a modernist ideal: the complete rationalization of architecture, wherein every design decision rested on a foundation of research and measure, wherein form was legitimated by appeal to the requirements of function and the facts of construction. All the factors of architectural invention were present in Cellophane House™, but rarely have they been so tirelessly scrutinized to discover even the finest detail about their nature in an effort to unveil potentialities usually overlooked by architects. Needless to say, Cellophane House™, for all its resolution, was knowingly provisional. Even as it was disassembled for storage, reuse, or recycling, so has it become a bundle of questions that are being put to subsequent projects in the office.

Tracing these research threads, both as practical responses to existing conditions and as independent, sustained research questions, explains a remarkable aspect of the firm's work: in addition to speculative projects such as Cellophane House™, they maintain a renovation practice that is simultaneously innovative and deeply sympathetic. It is not so much that the firm is respectful of older architecture; rather, they initiate a dialogue with existing buildings that is as intense, as detailed, as dogged, and as questioning as what they pursue for new buildings. Existing buildings are presumed to possess a range of capacities—embodied intelligence, so to speak—that are as powerful and multivalent as, say, the latest polymer composite building materials.

Having established an in-house instrument to generate a flow of research information, KieranTimberlake is constitutionally motivated to enhance, intensify, and to control that flow. Thus, at Loblolly House, for example, the architects installed a series of sensors to learn, long after the builders had left the site, how countless decisions regarding materials, orientation, fenestration, and so on, affected material movement, air pressure differentials, and temperature variations. How, in short, did the building behave as part of an environment rather than as an insular intervention? Similarly, sensors registered a range of thermal data both inside and out of Cellophane House™ as visitors scrambled through it by day and as it stood empty overnight. The flow of statistics gathered from these physical conditions has since rejoined other research streams at the firm's offices and will eventually find their way again into material form.

In turn, KieranTimberlake's dedication to research raises broad questions for architectural design practice today. Many architects aim their practices, in time-honored fashion, toward a series of declarations, one or another successful response to the always unique conditions of client and purpose, site, materials and construction, and to the particularities of a formal program. But today, with computer intelligence integral to design and manufacturing, not to mention delivery, construction, and maintenance, architecture has come more and more to resemble an ongoing flow of decisions regarding the entire lifecycle of a building. How might such a transformation in the central activity of design change architectural practice itself? For once, KieranTimberlake appears to have settled on an answer: an internal research engine that drives forward individual projects, which then set agendas for ensuing work. By constantly asking questions—outwardly toward materials, assemblies, entire buildings, and building lifecycles, and inwardly toward their own methods, reflexively adjusting their research even as they push it in new directions—KieranTimberlake has created a tool commensurate with the increasingly fluid nature of design in an age of computation and synthetic materials. They have learned how to manage what they call a project's "informational context," the torrents of knowledge regarding material properties, energy flows, functional considerations and spatial relations, budget decisions, physical contexts, and more, all of which combine to inform and condition the continuing creation of architecture in our own day.

Sandy Isenstadt

ALPHA

# BACK TO THE BEGINNING

**Two philosophies have** guided our work since the inception of our firm in 1984. The first: *build our ideas*. The second: *learn from them*. The latter was formalized when we became one of the few architecture firms to be certified by the International Standards Organization (ISO) in 2005. With this certification, we mapped and standardized processes, creating a management system that would keep us on a path of reflection and improvement. We are committed to this process—plan, do, monitor, learn—and start the process again, learning from each feedback loop.

In a sense, it has been easier to enact the second philosophy than the first. When our firm was young, fewer opportunities to build came our way. We made a conscious choice to stay away from competitions, since they rarely resulted in opportunities to build. We set out to make the most of every commission, no matter how small, and seized every opportunity to make real buildings. In time, a third philosophy emerged: *continue to build upon the initial ideas*. How might fresh thoughts come from working with the wonderful outcomes of our previous projects? How could they be combined in new ways and lead to better and innovative results? Cellophane House™ is an example of one such outcome.

In the spring of 2007 we received an invitation from Barry Bergdoll, the Chief Curator of Architecture and Design at The Museum of Modern Art (MoMA), to submit qualifications to participate in an upcoming show on prefabrication with the working title, *Home Delivery: New Horizons in Factory Made Architecture*. In the tradition of the "House in the Garden" series held at MoMA mid-century, the show would present full-scale designs that would reveal the current state and future potential of prefabricated architecture. What intrigued us was the opportunity to extend the conversation we had begun with our book, *refabricating Architecture*, by building a prototype that would explore several game-changing agendas established earlier on: the speed of on-site assembly, design for disassembly, and a holistic approach to the life cycles of materials.

The projects built were chosen after an initial consideration of some 500 architects and firms, from which 21 proposals were solicited. In less than three weeks after receiving the solicitation, we conceived of a design, began forming partnerships with builders and suppliers, and delivered a scheme and physical model to MoMA. Five schemes were ultimately selected for delivery to a site adjacent to the museum between 53rd and 54th Streets in Manhattan in July 2008. The whole process from selection to delivery took eleven months.

Timing is everything. Six months prior we completed Loblolly House, an off-site fabricated home on the Chesapeake Bay that confirmed theoretical positions drawn in *refabricating Architecture* by incorporating three-dimensional digital modeling and integrated component assemblies. The thousands of parts that make up a typical house were collapsed into a few dozen "elements" that were rapidly attached to a bolt-together "scaffold" of industrial aluminum. The elements were assembled off-site in a factory, and the house was assembled on-site in six weeks.

As important to building efficiently and swiftly on-site was that the architecture be united with its environment—in this case, a thin strip of waterfront land populated with tall, thin Loblolly Pines. The hybrid assembly methodology enabled the architecture to conform to its context, with massing, material selection, and placement of the house addressing site specificity. The customizable nature of the assembly means the same methodology can be applied for very different contexts.

After its completion, Loblolly House continued to provide us with valuable feedback. We monitored the temperatures in the house to verify that the west facade was passively heating and cooling as intended. We performed a virtual disassembly of the house, calculating its carbon footprint and the significant amount of embodied energy that could be captured if the house materials were repurposed in its next life. We embarked on a partnership with the developer LivingHomes on a mass-customizable housing product that employs similar hybrid building methodologies, and worked with Make It Right in New Orleans on sustainable, post-Katrina housing.

At the same time, we were seeking avenues to advance our development of SmartWrap™, a lightweight, energy gathering, mass customizable, and recyclable building envelope system. The first generation of SmartWrap™ speculated on organic photovoltaics (OPV) and organic light emitting diodes (OLED) deposition printed onto thin plastic film, creating a system of functional building layers on a single substrate. The product debuted at the Cooper-Hewitt, National Design Museum in 2003. We learned valuable lessons from the first exposition and continued its development. As we anticipated printed OPV and OLED technologies would be developed further for large-scale applications, we sought the opportunity to prototype SmartWrap™ on a larger scale.

Looking beyond the MoMA competition brief, it seemed to us that a single purpose, site-specific project would be only partially on target. What then were some of the goals, objectives, and queries this project might address? How would this house investigate mass-customization? What might its assembly portend about its disassembly and afterlife? Can we quantify the impact that the embodied energy of materials has on its carbon footprint? How might we refine the construction methodologies investigated in Loblolly House? Could we demonstrate a new future that might change the way the industry models, constructs, and delivers housing? And what should it be called?

The term *cellophane*, a material we grew up with, had a ring to it. What other name could a plastic, thinly wrapped residence have? Stephen Kieran's son Christopher once called Cellophane House™ the 'love-child' of SmartWrap™ and Loblolly House. We would add that it is also the progeny of *refabricating Architecture*, a willing and dedicated museum curator, and a cast of hundreds of collaborators. It took dedication, perseverance, ample time, and a lot of resources. We had fun. And we think it showed.

**Stephen Kieran and James Timberlake**

1.1   SmartWrap™ Pavilion, Cooper-Hewitt, National Design Museum, 2003

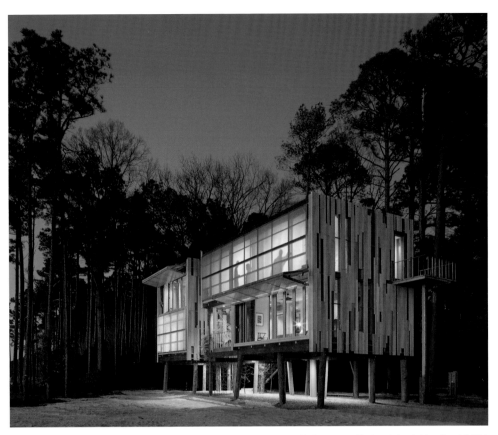

1.2   Loblolly House, Taylors Island, Maryland, 2006

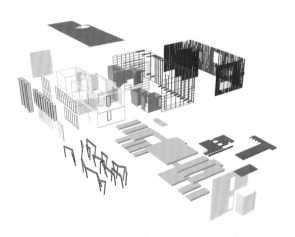

1.3   Loblolly House off-site fabricated elements

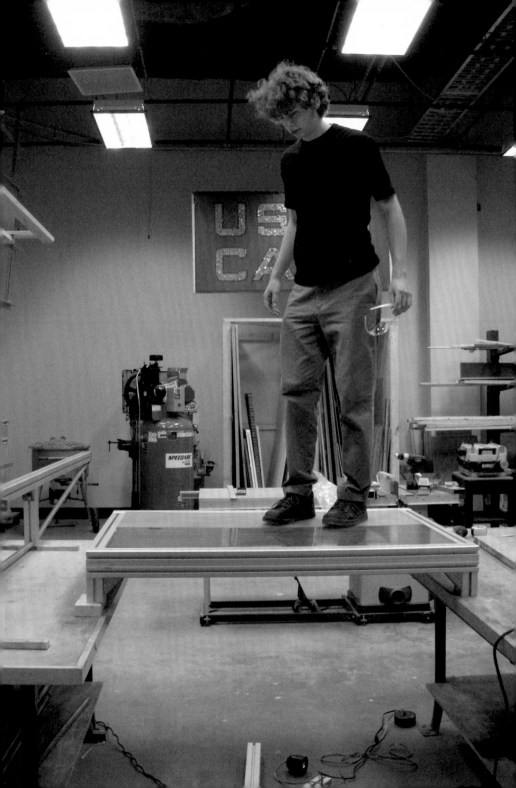

# CONCEPTION

# WHY A FIVE-STORY TRANSPARENT HOUSE?

**In the context** of an exhibition, where experimentation is expected, the marriage of the aluminum frame with its transparent Smart-Wrap™ skin offered possibilities to envision what it might be like to live transparently. While this phenomenon was addressed in the 20th century by projects such as Philip Johnson's Glass House, and today with the popularity of glass-clad condos in cities, we wanted to speculate on how a fully transparent, energy-gathering dwelling might be developed for the mass-market. Given the conventional materials that most houses are constructed with today, might employing an innovative, transparent building skin cause us and the exhibit goers to think differently about how we will live in the near future? How might this change the way we go about our lives on a daily basis?

The ability to adapt a house from urban to exurban to rural locations became a constraint to be explored. We wanted to challenge the perception that off-site fabricated architecture does not fit well into different contexts and that it cannot be used for tall, large-scale structures. In the context of introducing a completely new type of house to the marketplace, we selected a height and footprint that would provide a variety of program and product options not currently available. The five-story, 1800 square foot dimension we chose provided ample surface area to harness solar power via the building envelope, and integrate SmartWrap™ into a high performance wall that would form the transparent "ductwork" of the natural ventilation strategy of the house. Due to the strength of the frame, large open spans could be created, allowing us to literally "open up" options for off-site constructed housing and its tendency to privilege wall over window.

2.1   Competition model

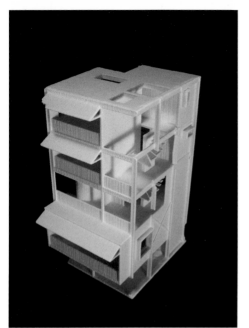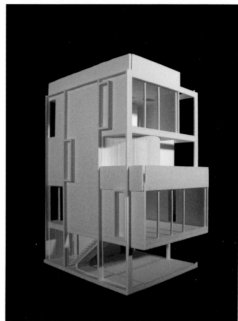

2.2   Early 3D printed models

2.3  Rendering

# WHAT IS A PARAMETRIC MODEL?

**The static drawing** types that architects have relied on since the Renaissance to communicate with builders and craftspeople are no longer sufficient to convey design intent for buildings today. Each drawing, be it a plan, section, or detail, exists as a separate artifact. Depicting even a small portion of a building in this way requires many drawings, and there are often critical connections that are not understood until the moment of construction. New digital tools enable architects to simulate full-scale buildings in three dimensions, thereby making the interaction of building elements fully visible and effectively closing the gaps inherent in two-dimensional representation.

Cellophane House™ was designed as a three-dimensional parametric model using Building Information Modeling (BIM) software. The parametric model contains all the information necessary for the development, fabrication, and assembly of the building. With the capability of being a shared working model, it provides the means for architects, engineers, planners, and fabricators to work in a more fully integrated environment. BIM yields more efficient structural and mechanical coordination, greater management of parts and schedules for procurement, a clearer approach to assembly sequencing, and a greater measure of control over fabrication and construction.

For Cellophane House™ we used BIM to design the building, but also to describe the building to fabricators and assemblers through isometric models, sequence drawings, and piece drawings. BIM is also what made it possible to build the house components simultaneously instead of sequentially. Materials could be prepared in advance to the required tolerances because dimensional discrepancies are reconciled virtually in the model rather than during construction. We were able to order the correct quantities of materials and provide exact dimensions to the suppliers to plan cuts well in advance of assembly.

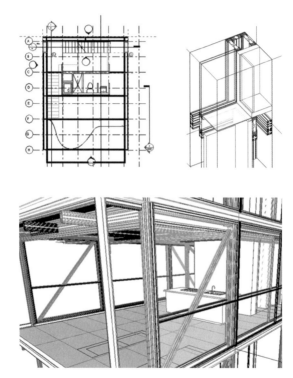

2.4   Screenshots of the BIM showing a plan, detail, and fully assembled view

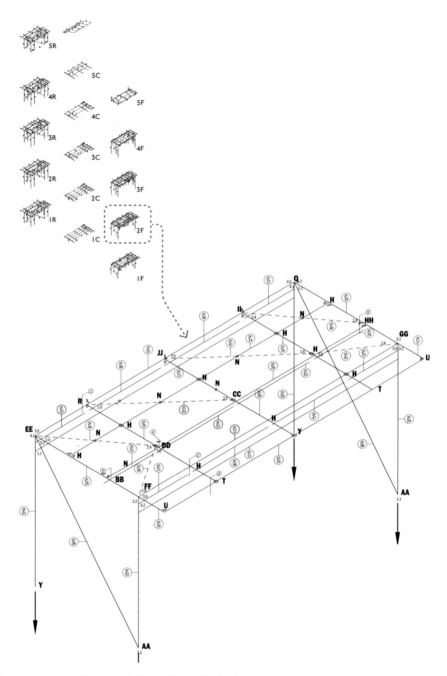

2.5  Piece drawings provide assembly instructions to the fabricators

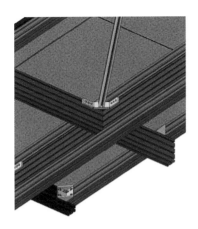

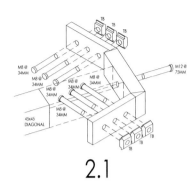

## 2.1

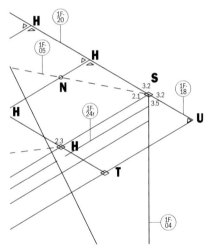

2.6   A BIM model, connector drawings, and piece drawings inform the physical assembly

# WHAT MATERIALS ARE USED IN CELLOPHANE HOUSE™?

**The desire to** minimize the total carbon embodied in Cellophane House™ led us in two directions in terms of material choice. First, we designed the house for disassembly and reuse of its constituent parts with the requirement that all the materials be part of existing recycling streams. Second, the materials needed to be lightweight to minimize embodied energy and reduce foundation costs.

The building skin is SmartWrap™ and glass, both highly recyclable materials. SmartWrap™ is made primarily of polyethylene tere-phthalate (PET), commonly used for portable drink containers. At just 3mm thick, it can cover a larger surface area with a minimal volume of material relative to glass curtain wall assemblies. This, combined with its light weight, results in a lower total embodied energy when compared to glass. Also due to its lightness, it can be erected in a fraction of conventional building time using less labor and smaller machinery. At the end of its useful life, it can be easily disassembled and fed into a recycling stream.

The building skin is attached to an aluminum structural frame that is also lightweight and recyclable. The interior floors, ceilings, and wall partitions are made of structural plastic, eliminating the need for additional structural framing. The translucent roof is made with modular polycarbonate panels that feature a standing seam connection method that snaps in place and requires no sealant or adhesives.

The weight vs. embodied energy equation for the building skin is a strong argument for the sustainability of lightweight, yet energy intensive building systems. For example, despite covering a similar amount of surface area, the weight of the PET in the structure is 594 lbs, with a carbon footprint of 1,386 lbs, while the weight of the glass is 10,685 lbs, with a carbon footprint of 8,548 lbs—600% higher than the PET. Although the embodied carbon for a pound of PET is three times that of glass, PET is the better option with respect to lowering the carbon footprint of the structure.

2.7   Stack of structural plastic flooring sheets

2.8   Translucent resin wall partition

2.9   Roll of polyethylene terephthalate (PET)

2.10   Section of aluminum framing

2.11   High strength steel bolts

2.12   Aluminum folding door kit

# HOW IS CELLOPHANE HOUSE™
# HELD TOGETHER?

**In striving for** permanence, conventional construction techniques fix materials to one another in such a way that they become composite elements, losing much of their identity as discrete materials. For example, a conventional hardwood floor consists of wood finished with polyurethane resin, nailed and glued to a plywood subfloor that is nailed and glued to a set of wood joists. The only way to separate the materials is to demolish them, a process as inelegant as it is wasteful.

By contrast, Cellophane House™ is assembled from discrete materials held in place by attachment methods that are quickly and easily reversible. The off-the-shelf aluminum structural frame provides the means to attach and eventually detach individual materials, allowing them to be easily extracted, exchanged, reused, or recycled.

Engineered and manufactured by Bosch Rexroth, the framing system was developed to construct enclosures and armatures for workplace equipment in factories. The framing members feature a T-shaped slot on each side that serves as the negative receptor for a variety of friction connections. Beams, columns, and accessories are fastened together with T-bolts rather than welds or adhesives, and are installed using a standard ratchet.

Most of the Cellophane House™ uses 45mm or 90mm gussets, along with Bosch spring clips, inside-to-inside gussets, and gusset plates, requiring anywhere from four to sixteen T-bolts to be secured into the channels of the extruded aluminum members. In addition to providing the mechanism for structural connections, the T-slot is used as a channel for concealing wiring and for operating the sliding doors within the house.

The standard Bosch connectors were not designed for the large gravity, wind, and seismic loads that develop in buildings. We supplemented them with several custom connectors developed with our structural engineer, adapting the system to meet the requirements of a free-standing, residential structure. The most creative of these, originally conceived at Loblolly House, uses a shear lug to transfer large gravity loads and is coupled with standard Bosch connectors to hold the connector against the frame. The system of connectors holistically resists live and dead loads and lateral forces, and fixes the building to the ground.

**BOLT**          **STACK**

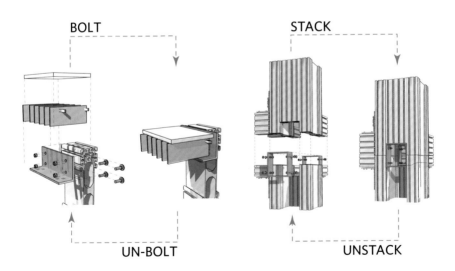

**UN-BOLT**          **UNSTACK**

2.13   Aluminum framing provides the means to fasten materials together with reversible connections

The wall partitions and floor panels are attached to the frame with 3M VHB (Very High Bond) tape, which structurally cross-bonds and gets stronger with time. The tape is simple to apply and securely fastens the polycarbonate panels and lights to the aluminum members. When the house was disassembled, the panels were pulled off and the tape was easily removed.

Cellophane House™ was anchored to the MoMA site on a grade beam of cast-in-place concrete, but any kind of foundation could work with simple modifications. In the process of designing the building we discussed alternative methods including mat footings, helical anchors, caissons, and piles. If designed for the correct wind loads, the house could even be attached to a pre-existing structure.

2.14   Wall partitions are taped to the aluminum frame

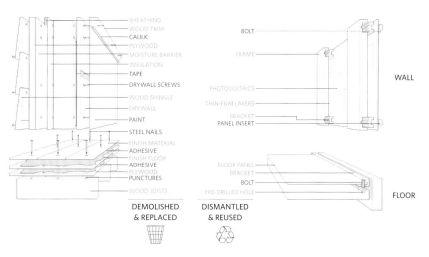

## PERMANENTLY FIXED

SHEATHING
WOOD TRIM
CAULK
PLYWOOD
MOISTURE BARRIER
INSULATION
TAPE
DRYWALL SCREWS
WOOD SHINGLE
DRYWALL
PAINT
STEEL NAILS
FINISH MATERIAL
ADHESIVE
FINISH FLOOR
ADHESIVE
PLYWOOD
PUNCTURES
WOOD JOISTS

**DEMOLISHED
& REPLACED**

## TEMPORARILY HELD

BOLT
FRAME

PHOTOVOLTAICS
THIN-FILM LAYERS
BRACKET
PANEL INSERT

WALL

FLOOR PANEL
BRACKET
BOLT
PRE-DRILLED HOLE

FLOOR

**DISMANTLED
& REUSED**

2.15   Construction vs. Assembly

2.16   The house is attached to the site with a cast-in-place concrete grade beam foundation

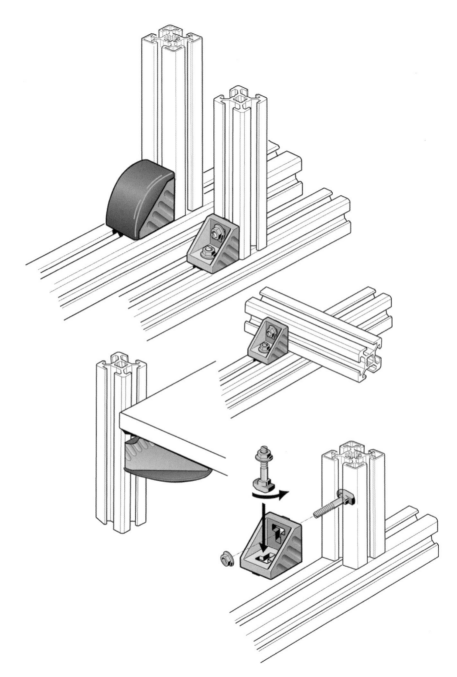

2.17   Diagram of aluminum members connected with gussets and T-bolts

2.18 Custom designed connector working in concert with off-the-shelf connectors

2.19 Custom connectors designed to meet the requirements of a free-standing structure

# WHAT ARE THE BENEFITS OF
# THE ALUMINUM FRAME?

**Beginning with off-the-shelf** materials, the point is not to re-invent a constructive strategy, but to explore the inventive possibilities of arranging and rearranging parts, and to capitalize on and extend the capacities of existing technologies. The Bosch Rexroth extruded aluminum frame is a pre-existing, readily available system with a well-established after market. The aluminum members are all pre-engineered, with clearly defined load capacities, giving them the high precision required for off-site fabrication, while keeping costs down and flexibility up.

Though it is high in embodied energy, aluminum will not rust or break down from exposure and needs no painting or finishing. It is lightweight, greatly reducing foundation costs, and has the durability, long life, and capability for reuse or recycling that offset the initial impact of production. Cellophane House™ uses 32,245 lbs of aluminum, all of which was reclaimed through the disassembly strategy.

2.20   A beam is bolted to a column with a series of custom connectors

# CAN OTHER MATERIALS BE USED?

**Cellophane House™ is** mass-customizable. It is a scaffold, an armature of parts that can be configured to meet specific needs or desires. Through simple modifications, the house can adapt to different site conditions, climatic factors, solar orientations, slopes, and adjacencies. Since all structural loads are carried by the frame, it is also simple to rearrange interior floor plans. Material options, easily substituted due to the ease of connection to the aluminum frame, allow the house to accommodate the needs, tastes, and budgets of a range of occupants.

Cellophane House™ is a prototype, intended to be provocative. Someone concerned with more practical needs and budgetary concerns might choose a quite different package of materials. Opaque panel materials, for instance, might replace the transparent wrapper, rendering the building solid and dense rather than light and ephemeral. Regardless of the changes that are made, the nature of the house remains the same: it is a matrix for the connection of materials.

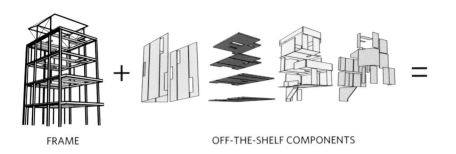

FRAME                 OFF-THE-SHELF COMPONENTS

$ ⟶ $$$

CUSTOMIZABLE OPTIONS:

SHELL           INTERIORS          SERVICES          EQUIPMENT

2.21   The house is mass-customizable to individual needs and transformable over time

# HOW IS SMARTWRAP™ MADE?

**SmartWrap™ is a** lightweight building envelope system that speculates on the integration of climate control, power, lighting, and information display on a polyethylene terephthalate (PET) substrate. Conceived and developed since 2000, we began deep research and development in 2002, collaborating with various industry partners to engineer and fabricate a prototype. During the development of the first prototype, we pursued emerging systems including phase change materials for temperature control; organic light emitting diodes (OLED), performing in conjunction with organic thin-film transistors for lighting and data display; and organic photovoltaic cells to power the OLED system. As there was no developed system for organic printing onto a large-scale, flexible substrate, it was necessary for the systems, except for the printed circuitry, to be adhered to the PET. A pavilion was created to demonstrate the prototype skin at the Cooper-Hewitt, National Design Museum SOLOS exhibition in 2003.

At Cellophane House™ we deployed SmartWrap™ on a much larger scale. To develop the next generation, we had to verify that certain technologies, unavailable five years earlier, had been sufficiently developed. Printed photovoltaics, one of the primary components we sought to use, were on the cusp of commercial development, but not yet ready for integration. By using commercially available, thin-film solar panels, affixed to the PET, we were able to demonstrate the highest level of current development.

The SmartWrap™ walls at Cellophane House™ are comprised of seventy-four panels, each containing four functioning layers stretched on an aluminum frame. The layers include a PET weather barrier, a PET layer with thin-film photovoltaic cells, a layer of infrared blocking film, and an interior PET layer. The panels were fabricated in Pennsylvania, using sophisticated methods of tensioning the PET to the extruded aluminum frames and adhering the thin-film PV cells and circuitry.

2.22   First SmartWrap™ prototype on display, 2003

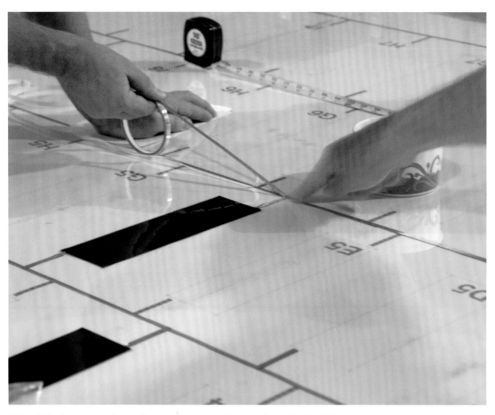

2.23    Thin-film photovoltaic cells and copper circuitry are adhered to the PET

2.24    PET is stretched to the aluminum frames

2.25   A stack of SmartWrap™ panels

2.26  Exterior detail of SmartWrap™ facade

2.27   SmartWrap™ panels enclosing the west facade

# HOW DOES THE CELLOPHANE HOUSE™ ENVELOPE PERFORM?

**We think of** the SmartWrap™ walls that enclose the Cellophane House™ as a filter that selectively lets in what we want (daylight and seasonal heat) but keeps out what we do not want (ultraviolet light and hot or cool air, depending on the season). The wall assembly is comprised of four layers of PET, one of which blocks infrared radiation. The depth of the vertical framing elements forms a two inch gap between the two innermost layers. The goal is to create a continuous convection current inside the gap, and selectively trap heat to warm the house or eject it to cool the house.

As conceived, the wall is an active ventilation system, using fans and dampers to move air. Fans can increase the flow of air, and dampers trap heat in the cavity or release heat through ventilating slots at the top of the wall. Since the house was only on view for three months in summer and fall seasons, we opted not to deploy the fans, but instead to focus on the effectiveness of the double-wall PET assembly. As prototyped at MoMA, the wall was a passive ventilation system operating through stack pressure, while the infrared blocking film played the primary role in managing temperatures within the house. Different sized window openings in the north and south walls assisted in the passive ventilation of the house. By manually adjusting the openings the pressure differential between the two window types could be exploited to create airflow.

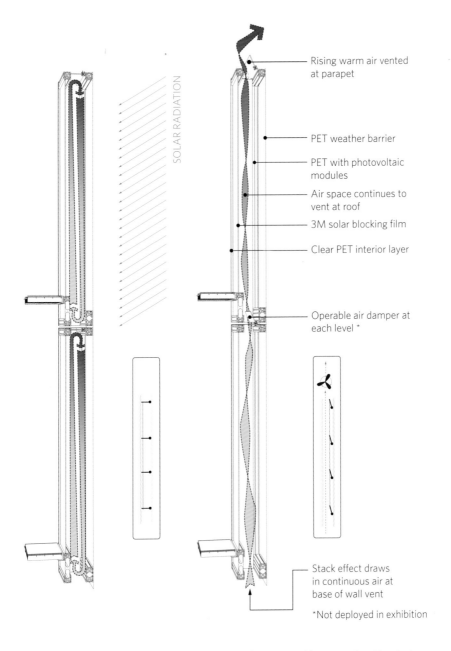

SOLAR RADIATION

Rising warm air vented
at parapet

PET weather barrier

PET with photovoltaic
modules

Air space continues to
vent at roof

3M solar blocking film

Clear PET interior layer

Operable air damper at
each level *

Stack effect draws
in continuous air at
base of wall vent

*Not deployed in exhibition

2.28   Wall section showing PET layers and air cavity with proposed venting strategy

2.29   Parallel opening windows open only slightly, causing a pressure
       differential that helps air circulate through the house

2.30    Folding glass doors on one side of the house provide natural ventilation

# HOW IS PERFORMANCE
# MEASURED?

**The challenge of** balancing climate and thermal comfort in an enclosed PET structure without traditional insulation required mining knowledge from our previous experience developing high performance building envelopes. These envelopes create new expectations for how building facades can function, proving they should not just provide insulation and protection from the elements, but offer the potential to regulate the building environment. Post-occupancy monitoring of our wall systems at Melvin J. and Claire Levine Hall at the University of Pennsylvania, the Yale University Sculpture Building, and Loblolly House provided a basis for speculation on how the Cellophane House™ facade might function, and prompted our decision to monitor the house during its three-month deployment at MoMA. The difference here was that, due to the short existence of the house, our resulting data set would be limited in comparison to data collected on permanent structures observed for longer durations across seasons. Being part of a continuous investigation, we deemed a small data set to be better than none. In the end, even the small data set provided enough hints for us to determine a direction for further research.

We monitored the thermal performance of the SmartWrap™ technology for three months from July to October. Because the house was in the shadow of much taller buildings for most of the day, sensors were placed on the west elevation, the only location with direct solar exposure. Self-contained pendant temperature sensors

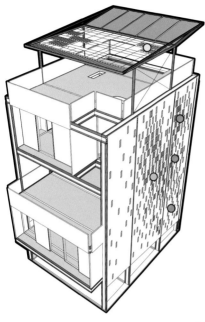

○ Solar radiation, ambient
temperature, and relative
humidity sensors

◉ Thermocouple and pendant
sensors

◒ Internal temperature and
relative humidity sensors

2.31    Sensor locations on the west facade and roof

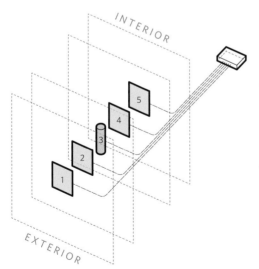

1. THERMOCOUPLE
   Measures exterior surface
   temperatures, reflecting ambient
   temperatures and heat gain

2. THERMOCOUPLE
   Measures rate of thermal transfer
   from interior to exterior

3. PENDANT SENSOR
   Measures the temperature of the
   air within the cavity

4. THERMOCOUPLE
   Monitors the degree to which the
   cavity space buffers the interior
   from exterior temperature

5. THERMOCOUPLE
   Measures the thermal transfer
   from the cavity to interior surface

2.32    Sensor types used to monitor temperatures within and around the wall assembly were suspended inside the cavities of the 2nd, 3rd, and 4th floors, logging data every thirty minutes. This data showed how the skin responded to large-scale patterns such as diurnal cycling and to smaller, more rapid events such as exposure to direct solar radiation and sudden drops in temperature caused by thunderstorms. Interior relative humidity and dry bulb temperature from the 3rd floor were monitored and logged; and exterior solar radiation, ambient temperatures, and relative humidity were recorded from a roof-mounted weather station. A digital anemometer was used to analyze airspeed within the cavity of the building envelope.

Rather than draw solid conclusions from the data, our monitoring exercise raised further questions and brought certain aspects into focus for further investigation. These include deepening our understanding of the physics of how infrared blocking film interacts with sunlight, a study of the correlations between sun angle and the transmission of solar radiation energy, and strategies to improve insulation in a lightweight structure with low thermal mass.

We were relieved and intrigued to discover that the house kept relatively cool throughout the hot, humid summer. This was due in part to the low thermal mass of the structure which allowed it to cool down rapidly and fully at night. The fact that it did not overheat during periods of peak sunlight points to the effectiveness of the thermal buffering in the double-layer SmartWrap™ wall system, and the efficacy of infrared shielding and natural ventilation.

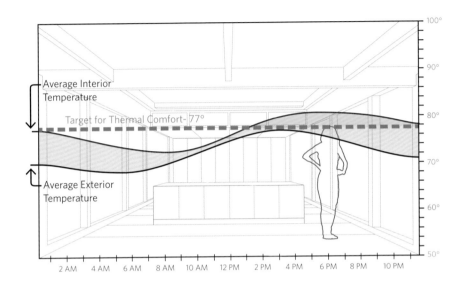

Average Interior
Temperature

Target for Thermal Comfort- 77°

Average Exterior
Temperature

100°
90°
80°
70°
60°
50°

2 AM   4 AM   6 AM   8 AM   10 AM   12 PM   2 PM   4 PM   6 PM   8 PM   10 PM

2.33   Composite average of interior and exterior temperatures
(July-October) compared to thermal comfort target

# ASSEMBLY

# WHAT IS THE ASSEMBLY PROCESS?

**Cellophane House™ is** assembled like a car—the whole construction is broken down into integrated assemblies to ease shipping and construction on site. These integrated assemblies, called chunks, are fabricated off site simultaneously, making the assembly of each individual component independent from other components. Each chunk contains the aluminum structure, floor, and external walls. Once delivered to the site, the chunks are stacked one atop the other with a crane. At MoMA there were nine chunks: one front and one rear for each level, and one flat panel in between linking the front and rear chunks. The weight of each chunk was calculated to plan how they should be rigged, and the parametric model was used to plan and describe the assembly sequence to the riggers.

Chunks are typically broken down even further into sub-assemblies. One example of a sub-assembly is a stud wall. While a traditional stud wall can take weeks to construct if it is built in succession, trade by trade, the partitions and panels in Cellophane House™ took just a few days to assemble. Another example is the five-story, structural acrylic stair, which was fabricated at a separate factory in five sections and installed into the chunks prior to delivery to the site. Each section was mounted on Bosch structural members and nestled into the frame. Other sub-assemblies include the Smart-Wrap™ panels and the bathroom pods.

The chunking strategy shifts a great deal of the assembly to the factory from the field. While it enhances the speed in the field, it places an extraordinary premium on precision. In general the chunks aligned well one to the next, with one exception, which stopped the field assembly work for a day until the source of the problem could be identified and fixed.

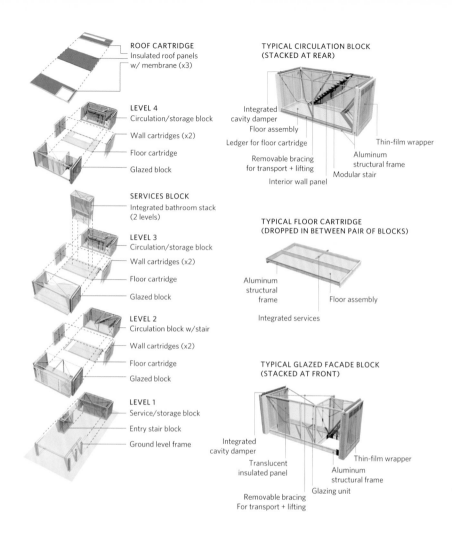

**ROOF CARTRIDGE**
Insulated roof panels
w/ membrane (x3)

**TYPICAL CIRCULATION BLOCK
(STACKED AT REAR)**

Integrated
cavity damper
Floor assembly
Ledger for floor cartridge
Thin-film wrapper
Removable bracing
for transport + lifting
Aluminum
structural frame
Modular stair
Interior wall panel

**LEVEL 4**
Circulation/storage block

Wall cartridges (x2)

Floor cartridge

Glazed block

**SERVICES BLOCK**
Integrated bathroom stack
(2 levels)

**LEVEL 3**
Circulation/storage block

Wall cartridges (x2)

Floor cartridge

Glazed block

**TYPICAL FLOOR CARTRIDGE
(DROPPED IN BETWEEN PAIR OF BLOCKS)**

Aluminum
structural
frame
Floor assembly

Integrated services

**LEVEL 2**
Circulation block w/stair

Wall cartridges (x2)

Floor cartridge

Glazed block

**TYPICAL GLAZED FACADE BLOCK
(STACKED AT FRONT)**

**LEVEL 1**
Service/storage block

Entry stair block

Ground level frame

Integrated
cavity damper
Thin-film wrapper
Translucent
insulated panel
Aluminum
structural frame
Glazing unit
Removable bracing
For transport + lifting

3.2   Early conceptual chunk assembly diagram utilizing cartridges and blocks

3.3 Chunks on the assembly line at Kullman Buildings Corp.

3.4 Building a wall sub-assembly

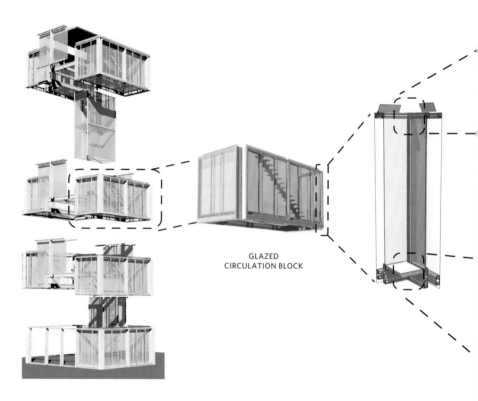

GLAZED
CIRCULATION BLOCK

ASSEMBLY

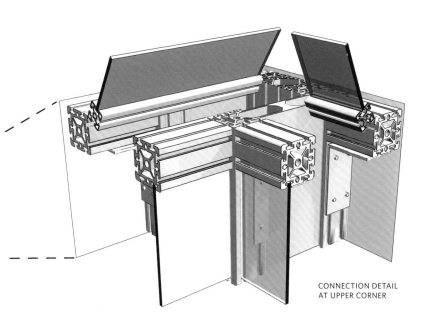

CONNECTION DETAIL
AT UPPER CORNER

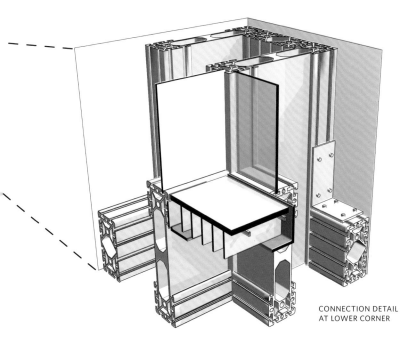

CONNECTION DETAIL
AT LOWER CORNER

3.5   Early conceptual detail drawing

## Off-site assembly schedule

WEEK 1  Design work complete
95% of the materials ordered
SmartWrap™ fabrication begins
Full-scale mockup 100% complete
Structural material for two chunks delivered

WEEK 2  Stair mockup reviewed and approved
Stair treads and wall panels fabricated
Steel connectors fabricated
Steel connectors epoxy coated
Holes tapped and countersunk in aluminum extrusions

WEEK 3  Acrylic stair fabrication continues
Steel connectors and structural bolts delivered
Structural frame assembly begins
Plumbing fixtures delivered
LED fixtures delivered

WEEK 4  Floor material cut to size
Construction and shop drawings complete
Remaining 5% materials ordered

WEEK 5  Chunk 1R assembly begins
Polycarbonate roof material delivered to factory

WEEK 6  First floor stair delivered to factory
Structural framing for chunks 1R and 2R complete
Structural framing for chunks 1C and 1F underway
Fabrication of curtainwall angles underway
Tensioning of SmartWrap™ wall panels tested

WEEK 7  Glass curtainwall arrives at factory
Structural framing for chunks 1F, 1C, and 2F complete
Additional aluminum extrusions are delivered
LED light fixtures and flooring installed in completed chunks 1R, 2R, 1C, and 1F
Interior partition panels are cut and prepared for installation

WEEK 8  Chunk 2R set on top of 1R to test stacking strategy

|          | Three levels of structural framing complete |
|          | Interior partitions are assembled |
|          | Stair installed into chunks 1R and 2R |
| WEEK 9   | Windows installed |
|          | Bathroom pods arrive from UK |
|          | Panels attached to partition walls |
|          | Stair installation on chunks 1R and 2R complete |
|          | Steel connectors that support the structure are installed |
|          | Floor panels dry-fitted in all chunks |
|          | Final aluminum extrusions prepared |
|          | Rain water leader fabricated |
|          | Smartwrap™ panels fabricated |
|          | Aluminum grating for walkways, balconies, and roof fabricated |
| WEEK 10  | Interior partitions installed |
|          | Light fixtures installed |
|          | Curtainwall support angles installed |
| WEEK 11  | Last order of aluminum delivered |
|          | Stair installed into chunks 3R and 4R |
|          | Gutters fabricated |
|          | Plumbing installed in bathroom pods |
|          | Floor panels secured in all chunks |
|          | Schüco E² glazing installed on first two levels |
|          | SmartWrap™ frames installed |
|          | Concrete grade beams poured at site |
| WEEK 12  | All chunks fully assembled at the factory |
|          | Metal grating on roof deck installed |
|          | Light fixture distribution cable installed |
|          | Translucent roof canopy installed |
|          | Danpalon drainage system assembled |
|          | Ventilation louvers installed in partitions |
| WEEK 13  | Final connections on all chunks complete |
|          | Chunks moved to trucks for delivery |

# HOW WAS CELLOPHANE HOUSE™ DELIVERED?

**Each pre-assembled chunk**, representing an 80% completed element of the house, was transported individually from the factory to the site on a lowboy trailer. The factory is equipped with overhead gantry cranes for lifting the chunks. They were covered with heavy tarps and rested on temporary wood blocking, which aided in lifting them off the ground while protecting them from damage and stabilizing them in transit. Bracing plates and temporary shoring anchored directly on the trailers assured alignment and stability as they were lifted from the trailer.

The trailers were spaced thirty minutes to one hour apart to allow the loading to take place in shifts. Clearance limits for bridges and tunnels, and local and federal Department of Transportation laws, were taken into account to orchestrate the delivery. New Jersey has a law which prohibits oversized loads from traveling on their roads at night, while New York has a law prohibiting oversized loads from traveling during the day. This required all trucks to park on the New Jersey side of the George Washington Bridge before nightfall and cross the bridge into New York before daybreak.

The interior wall partitions, which are the equivalent of stud walls in a traditional dwelling, were shipped as separate elements and installed after the chunks were stacked, while the bathroom pods were installed on the center chunk prior to shipping. The bathroom pods slipped into the frame with fractional tolerances, demonstrating the precision achieved with the parametric model.

3.6   Chunk lifted by overhead gantry crane in factory

3.7   The exhibition site prior to assembly

3.8   Tarp covered chunks on trailer on Sixth Avenue in Manhattan

# DID CELLOPHANE HOUSE™ ASSEMBLE AS EXPECTED?

**In general, the** entire frame and chunks went together as planned, with 80% of the work completed in six days. The last 20% took an additional eight days and included installation of the exterior building skin panels, interior partition walls, glazing, and kitchen cabinetry.

Before going on site we tested the stacking of two chunks in the factory. Slide-in T-bars secured to the columns of the top chunk slid into the channels in the columns of the chunk below. Each of the twelve columns had between six and eight bars that had to align and be screwed in place to connect the two chunks—not an easy task when the chunks are suspended from a crane several stories high.

On site the first five chunks went together as expected, but when the sixth chunk was raised, it did not align properly. We discovered that the center vertical diagonal bracing was fabricated one inch too short, causing the entire chunk to be slightly compressed and two of its columns to be out of alignment. As soon as the diagonal brace was released, the columns moved back into place and the T-bars slid freely into the columns below. From then on, the remainder of the chunks went together smoothly. Fortunately, we worked with a crew of resourceful riggers who improvised a modified steel connector on the spot with pieces of scrap steel welded to the brace connection. Professional riggers, normally minor players in construction, were central to the on-site assembly process.

The relationship of digital to material precision proved to be a challenge because of the exact tolerances required for construction. Since Cellophane House™ is not repetitive in its dimensions, we had to design ten variations of angle connectors, sometimes differing by only a degree or two. This made it necessary to clearly label each connector to differentiate similar angles. Furthermore, the steel angle connectors required extreme precision to match up with the engineered Bosch aluminum. To streamline the design for the greater marketplace it would be important to minimize the number of diagonal connectors.

3.9    The first chunk is lowered onto the foundation

3.10  The front chunk is placed on the second level

3.11  Chunk with integrated SmartWrap™ and stair sub-assemblies is lifted into position

3.12   Fourth floor rear chunk is lifted by crane

3.13   The chunk is aligned and secured in place

3.14   View within the structure as chunks are stacked

3.15   Final fit-out of the exterior panels in progress

3.16   The superstructure is complete in six days

# WHAT IS A BATHROOM POD?

**Bathrooms and kitchens** are prime candidates for off-site fabrication because they are system intensive and require the sequencing of more trades requiring more time in smaller areas than any other space in buildings. In dwellings where there are numerous bathrooms, using off-site fabricated modules improves one of the most troubling aspects of construction sequencing.

Cellophane House™ has two 6' x 8' bathroom pods, each with an outer shell constructed of glass-reinforced plastic (GRP) and connected to a steel frame. They are outfitted with plumbing fixtures and bathroom accessories, ceiling and wall finishes, and light fixtures. The bathroom pods are installed onto the center chunks at the factory, which are delivered to the site on flat bed trucks and hoisted into place by a crane.

The bathroom pods are one example of how selecting a product in lieu of designing and fabricating anew can drastically reduce the cost and time involved in constructing a house. They were designed by Hopkins Architects in the UK for a project at Rice University. The GRP walls were fabricated in the UK and the pods were built and distributed in the US.

3.17　Interior view of bathroom pod with pre-installed plumbing, fixtures, and lighting

3.18　GRP bathroom pod shell

3.19   Bathroom pod wrapped in blue tarp prepared for lifting into position

3.20    Bathroom pod on center chunk craned into position

# HOW ARE THE ACRYLIC STAIRS MADE?

**Cellophane House™ has** five flights of stairs, each with fourteen treads and weighing 4,000 lbs. No epoxy or resin is used to assemble the stairs, nor is any hardware used to set them in place. The treads interlock with the adjacent wall panels using a mortise and tenon fastening system, a classic joint usually employed in wood construction. A notched sill plate at the horizontal joints between chunks keeps the stairs in alignment.

The stairs were designed with computer generated models and fabricated using digital CNC (computerized numeric control) routers. They were fabricated in Maryland and delivered to the factory in New Jersey for installation.

We decided to illuminate the treads after realizing through calculations and prototyping that the light from the walls was insufficient under different weather conditions and time of day. The lights were embedded in a notch under the treads, which provided a beautiful glow in the stairwell. The fabricator ran the power cords within the wall chamber of the stair panels before sealing the wall cavity, minimizing the need for on-site electrical work.

During the design of the stair we worked closely with the fabricator, the structural engineer and the assemblers to plan how the flights would be stacked. The notches in the sill plates had to be perfectly aligned before each chunk could be set in place. We devised a method of suspending the chunks from temporary rigging plates made from steel connectors attached to the aluminum beams. The chunks were moved by crane and suspended slightly above the joint, and a turnbuckle was used to make the micro-scale adjustments to steer them into exact position. The handrails were attached later in full, 18'–20' lengths.

3.21   LED and natural light cause the stairwell to glow

3.22　Mockup to test lighting of individual stair treads　　3.23　Stairs are lit by LEDs under each tread

3.24 Chunk containing stair sub-assembly is lowered on site

# HOW IS THE HOUSE ILLUMINATED?

**During the day** there is more than enough natural light diffusing through the walls, ceilings, and floors to illuminate the house without artificial lighting. One of the challenges with installing artificial lighting in a transparent house is concealing the wiring, which typically runs behind floors and walls. Slots in the aluminum members are a perfect pathway for integrating the lighting and channeling wires, and are capped with a protective cover that blends into the aluminum structure. The use of line voltage LED sources allows us to connect one hundred units on a single circuit, providing light to a complete floor without hidden transformers. Unlike lighting installed into soffits, it is flexible and can be moved like track lighting.

The lighting scheme is designed to work with the transparent and translucent building materials, while acknowledging the modularity of the structure. LEDs illuminate the surfaces of the house in various distributions, intensities, and colors. The structural plastic ceilings and floors are the diffusers of light throughout the house. The floors are up-lit with dimmable linear line voltage LED modules, which have a similar color of light (2800k) as household incandescent lighting, but are about twice as efficient. Further, the up-lighting allows a portion of the light to be reflected from the ceiling back down into the space in a soft and diffused manner, while creating a luminous plane to walk on.

The ground level and roof deck feature color changing LEDs, a reference to the days when only colored light could be produced with

LED technology. They provide a visual counterpoint to the mono-chromatic, warm white light of the middle stories. These differential layers are tied together with a digital lighting control system that allows the house to have an automated response cycle.

3.25    The house lit at night with high-efficiency LEDs

3.26  Wires are channeled through T-slots in the aluminum structure

3.27    The floors are up-lit with some of the light reflecting back down from the ceiling

EXHIBITION

4.1   Completed house on 53rd Street next to the American Folk Art Museum

4.2   House filled with museum patrons at dusk

4.3  View of entry vestibule through SmartWrap™ wall

4.4   Entry vestibule and stair from the carport to the first level

4.5  Abundant daylight fills the living spaces

4.6 Five flights of stairs lead from the entry to the roof terrace

4.7    Translucent stair and floor lit with LEDs create a luminous plane to walk on

4.8   Photovoltaic cells are located on the canopy and the SmartWrap™ wall cavity is vented at the roof

4.9   Third level bedroom and bathroom

4.10   Foldaway doors on the front of the house provide natural ventilation

4.11 Balconies and a roof terrace open the house to the outdoors

4.12    North facade glazing detail

4.13   Roof terrace detail

4.14   SmartWrap™ detail

4.15    Illuminated house in front of Eero Saarinen's CBS/Black Rock Building

DISASSEMBLY

# HOW WAS CELLOPHANE HOUSE™ REMOVED FROM THE SITE?

**Key considerations for** disassembly are the distance between sites, site access, and the availability of factory facilities for reassembly. While it seems most efficient to keep as much of the construction intact as possible, lowering factory requirements in the new location, total disassembly can be a better option if the structure is to travel a great distance because the materials can be more efficiently packed and transported.

We considered two possible scenarios for removing the house from the site. These options were influenced by the fact that we did not have a new site to move it to and needed to place the house in storage. The first scenario involved keeping the chunks intact and carting them away on flat bed trucks. The second scenario involved deglazing the house, un-stacking and placing the separated chunks on the ground, disassembling them at grade, and carefully storing the pieces for later reassembly. We chose the latter option because it offered multiple possibilities for future reassembly and allowed us to evaluate the full potential of the design for disassembly intent. It also minimized storage volume.

To calculate the cost of each option, we performed a virtual disassembly down to the removal of individual bolts. In each scenario, systems were either completely or partially disassembled before removal from the building, and we identified which aspects of disassembly influenced the cost of labor, materials, transportation, and storage. An important cost consideration was that the disassembly process for the chunks could not occur in as orderly and timely a fashion as it did for the assembly, resulting in a higher estimate for crane and rigging time. We decided to optimize crane time by lowering the chunks to a surrounding staging area for further disassembly.

The site was zoned to create adequate space for work, storage, and staging of building components. During the preparation stage, a sample of building components was removed from the building to the appropriate place in the staging area. Once the chunks were loosened, a crane "flew" them to designated locations on site, where they were disassembled and parts were segregated. The process was in some sense a reversal of the assembly, but without the level surface, controlled environment, and equipment found in the factory. Instead of the cranes used in the factory, we accomplished our work with a small forklift. Because the chunks are quite light, the forklift held them remarkably well despite their unusual size.

After the house was fully disassembled, the parts were organized neatly on pallets and removed from the site in two days. The only remnant of our time there was a patch of gravel in an asphalt lot.

5.1   The glass is removed and packed in crates fabricated on site

5.2 Glazing is removed to provide access to bolts

5.3    Disassembly crew removes bolts at chunk joints

5.4   Chunk is lowered to the ground by crane

5.5   Chunks are lined up at grade for disassembly with basic hand tools

5.6   Chunk is light enough to be moved with a forklift

# WHAT TYPE OF DOCUMENTATION WAS USED FOR DISASSEMBLY?

**The disassembly process** revealed the need to rigorously document as-built conditions if the building is to be reassembled in the same configuration. Even in the case of a well-planned, parametrically modeled project, there were some moments of improvisation during fabrication and assembly. Therefore, the system we devised to identify the parts and their respective locations in the house had to come from the synthesis of the digital construction documents and observations made on site during the disassembly.

Determining a method for tracking over 3,000 building components was itself a lesson in design strategy. While some components were already manually labeled from the factory assembly phase, the great majority were not. In this scenario all of the house parts were inventoried and labeled by hand using an ID tag. The tag contains a part ID, manufacturer information, location in the structure, and storage location. At the outset we projected three days for labeling all of the parts, but in reality it took six weeks because many were awkward to reach or inaccessible until the house was partially disassembled.

This suggests the great potential of BIM to generate a part identification system, enabling the direct transfer of this information at the time of fabrication through bar codes or radio-frequency identification. The identification system would be integral to the building rather than a post-assembly application.

5.7   Each component is labeled

GLA-1R-1.1

GLASS
PAF IGU
PACK GROUP    C6

5.8   Over 3,000 labels identify parts,
location, and packing information

5.9   Framing elements are sorted and bundled
according to type

# HOW WAS CELLOPHANE HOUSE™ PACKED AND STORED?

**To make reassembly** easier we initially considered palletizing the disassembled aluminum framing based on its location in the house, grouping the parts according to chunk. But this would have resulted in inefficiently packed pallets with many different sized members. Instead, we palletized the aluminum members based on size and length, which allowed us to load all of the structural framing for the entire house onto a single flatbed. All of the other house parts were palletized by type as well.

While the building was still standing, we estimated the weight and volume of all components so that the number and size of trucks to move the house could be accurately planned. The entire house was packed onto three flatbed trucks and two dry vans.

5.10  Wall partitions labeled and stacked

5.11  Aluminum framing arranged by size on pallets

5.12  Glazing is crated and loaded onto flatbed

5.13 Aluminum loaded on flatbed

5.14   Dry van interior during packing process

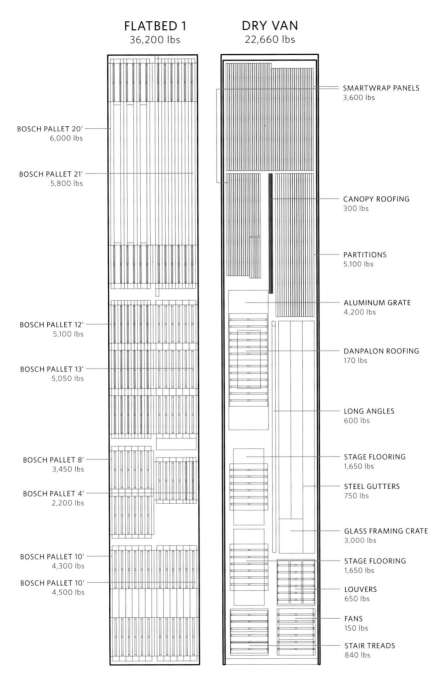

## FLATBED 1
### 36,200 lbs

## DRY VAN
### 22,660 lbs

BOSCH PALLET 20'
6,000 lbs

BOSCH PALLET 21'
5,800 lbs

BOSCH PALLET 12'
5,100 lbs

BOSCH PALLET 13'
5,050 lbs

BOSCH PALLET 8'
3,450 lbs

BOSCH PALLET 4'
2,200 lbs

BOSCH PALLET 10'
4,300 lbs

BOSCH PALLET 10'
4,500 lbs

SMARTWRAP PANELS
3,600 lbs

CANOPY ROOFING
300 lbs

PARTITIONS
5,100 lbs

ALUMINUM GRATE
4,200 lbs

DANPALON ROOFING
170 lbs

LONG ANGLES
600 lbs

STAGE FLOORING
1,650 lbs

STEEL GUTTERS
750 lbs

GLASS FRAMING CRATE
3,000 lbs

STAGE FLOORING
1,650 lbs

LOUVERS
650 lbs

FANS
150 lbs

STAIR TREADS
840 lbs

5.15   Truck packing plans for transport and storage

# WAS ANY MATERIAL WASTED?

**The materials for** the house were selected not only on the basis of physical properties, but also on the basis of their capacity for reuse and recycling. The house suffered certain inevitable wear and tear after months of heavy visitor traffic, environmental exposure, and a few mishaps during disassembly; but our initial thesis held up through the disassembly process, and virtually no waste was generated. All materials were easily separated and sorted using conventional carpentry tools, maintaining their integrity for recycling or future reuse.

The amount of energy embodied in a building's materials can be as high as or higher than the amount of energy it will consume over its forty-year life cycle. This indicates that to achieve true net zero buildings, an end-of-life material recovery strategy must be planned for in the building's design. We knew the exact measurements of the house materials, and performed an embodied energy analysis of the Cellophane House™, finding an intensity of 861 kWh per square foot. This figure, when compared to current energy intensity benchmarks, reveals that embodied energy is a significant contributor to its lifetime energy profile. The Cellophane House™ disassembly effort successfully recovered 100% of the energy embodied in materials, demonstrating the potential of this system to significantly reduce carbon emissions by extending the life cycle of materials.

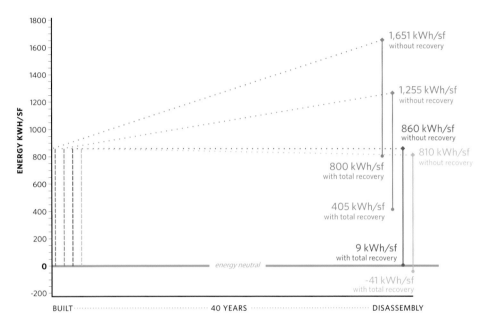

ENERGY KWH/SF

1800

1,651 kWh/sf
without recovery

1600

1400

1,255 kWh/sf
without recovery

1200

1000

860 kWh/sf
without recovery

810 kWh/sf
without recovery

800

800 kWh/sf
with total recovery

600

405 kWh/sf
with total recovery

400

200

9 kWh/sf
with total recovery

0                    energy neutral

-41 kWh/sf
with total recovery

-200

BUILT · · · · · · · · · · · · · · · · · · · · · · · · · · · · 40 YEARS · · · · · · · · · · · · · · · · · · · · · · · DISASSEMBLY

Current NE Source Energy Intensity US Energy Information Administration Bldg, 20 kWh/sf-year
Current (60%) 2030 Target Bldg, 10 KWh/sf-year
2030 Target Bldg, 0 kWh/sf-year
Best Department of Energy energy positive Bldg, -1.24 kWh/sf-year

- - - - Materials Embodied
· · · · · Operations
——— Disassembly

5.16    Comparison of embodied and operational energy in
        four buildings over forty years, with and without
        recovery of embodied energy through disassembly

| COMPONENT | FRAME | SKIN | GLAZING | WALL PANELS |
|---|---|---|---|---|
| MATERIAL |  Bosch Aluminum Framing <br> Steel Connectors <br> Steel Bolts |  SmartWrap™ (PET) <br> Aluminum Louvers |  Schüco Glass <br>  Schüco Aluminum Frame |  3form Varia (PETG) |
| TOTAL EMBODIED ENERGY | 955,631 kWh | 22,224 kWh | 71,423 kWh | 22,577 kWh |
| PERCENT RECOVERED | 99.99% | 100% | 100% | 100% |
| EMBODIED ENERGY RECOVERED | 954,675 kWh | 22,224 kWh | 71,423 kWh | 22,577 kWh |

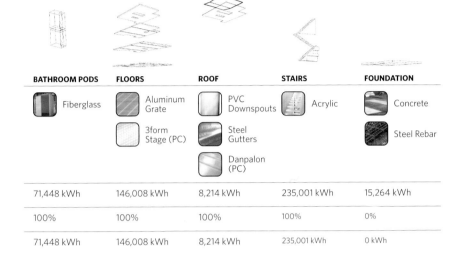

| BATHROOM PODS | FLOORS | ROOF | STAIRS | FOUNDATION |
|---|---|---|---|---|
| Fiberglass | Aluminum Grate | PVC Downspouts | Acrylic | Concrete |
| | 3form Stage (PC) | Steel Gutters | | Steel Rebar |
| | | Danpalon (PC) | | |
| 71,448 kWh | 146,008 kWh | 8,214 kWh | 235,001 kWh | 15,264 kWh |
| 100% | 100% | 100% | 100% | 0% |
| 71,448 kWh | 146,008 kWh | 8,214 kWh | 235,001 kWh | 0 kWh |

### TOTALS FOR 1,800 sf

| | |
|---|---|
| **TOTAL EMBODIED ENERGY** | 1,547,790 kWh 860 kWh/sf |
| **PERCENT RECOVERED** | 98.95% |
| **EMBODIED ENERGY RECOVERED** | 1,531,570 kWh 851 kWh/sf |

5.17   Total embodied energy recovered through disassembly

# WHAT MAKES CELLOPHANE HOUSE™ DIFFERENT FROM OTHER OFF-SITE FABRICATIONS?

**While many prefabricated** designs succeed in breaking down a building into modules that can be quickly joined together to make a building, this is still conventional construction, except it is construction in a factory as opposed to the building site. Such approaches typically embody a top-down prefabrication strategy: design the building, and then devise a system to make it work.

The design of Cellophane House™ evolved as a bottom-up approach. It began with the system as its basis, allowing architecture to grow out of its opportunities and constraints. What emerges from such a process is a design that is holistic in its approach, irreducible in its makeup.

A common perception of off-site fabricated housing is that originality and site specificity are lost in the manufacturing process. Throughout development of the design, we tried to eliminate conventional circumstances where a single design solution is applied to a unique scenario. Instead we designed a system of building that has a flexible set of rules that enable multiple outcomes.

While the "scaffold," or frame, helps accomplish our goals, it presents a unique set of challenges. Since it is left exposed and there is no drywall, molding, or veneer to "hide" imperfections, an extremely high level of precision is required. Furthermore, each design decision has to consider the totality of issues: ease of assembly, shipping method, assembly sequence, structural integrity, and disassembly method.

The experience of managing construction differed greatly in this project. In conventional construction the architect submits plans to the construction manager, who interprets the architect's intention with subcontractors and creates a separate set of shop drawings. The contractor and subcontractors procure and assign materials, and details are often worked out in the field. In this case we supplied the shop drawings, procured and assigned the materials, and provided step-by-step assembly diagrams.

As a result very little changed between the drawings and the finished project. If the building industry could achieve this marriage of intention with execution on a grander scale, then design and construction might move forward from its present byzantine systems and compromised outcomes towards greater control and craft for all building types and scales.

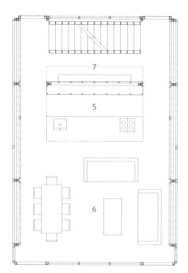

Second floor

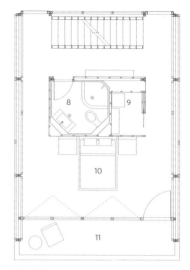

Third floor

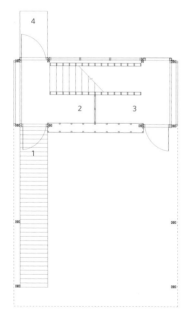

First floor

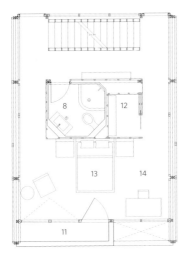

Fourth floor

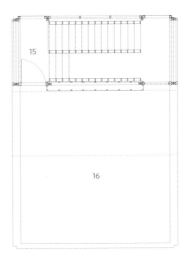

Fifth floor

1 Entry
2 Storage closet
3 Mechanical
4 ADA access
5 Kitchen
6 Living/Dining Room
7 Pantry
8 Bathroom pod
9 Master storage
10 Master bedroom
11 Balcony
12 Laundry
13 Second bedroom
14 Study
15 Mezzanine
16 Roof terrace

5.18   Floor plans

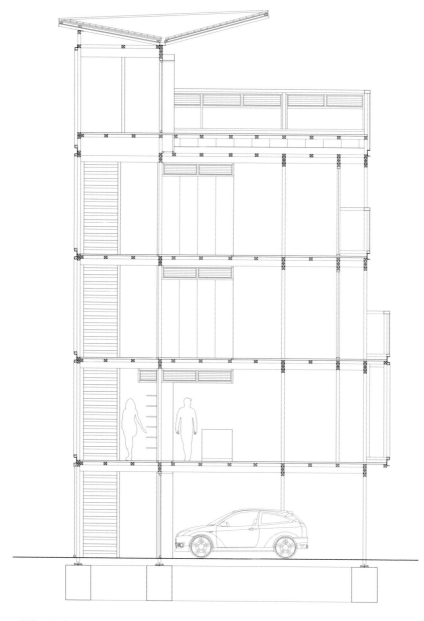

5.19　North-south section

5.20  East-west section

OMEGA

# FUTURE REDUX

**Shortly after the** opening of *Home Delivery* we received inquiries from individuals who were interested in purchasing Cellophane House™. Over fifty offers were received, some involving sites in New Mexico, Connecticut, and an unknown location in Russia. Some wanted an entirely new house; some had to have the one from the MoMA lot because of its provenance as an artifact. Some wanted to capitalize on the success of the exhibition; others were intrigued by the materiality of the house. At the end of the show we formally offered it for sale, advertising it in the *Wall Street Journal*, and word spread by mouth and the blog-o-sphere.

Our interest was in relocating it to a site that would offer potential to further monitor and measure real results. It was late 2008, and the country was in the midst of a credit crisis. Serious buyers began to rethink their plans. Unfortunately, none of the purchase offers combined the right amount of net benefit, opportunity, and reimbursement for our significant investment and intellectual property. So without a new site for the home, the 'love-child' was moved to a storage facility in New Jersey.

Was this a disappointment? Yes. Were we forlorn? No. Cellophane House™ is a prototype, a beginning from which more is to be learned. We continue to harbor great hope for producing more houses like it, and we have faith in its potential. By virtue of its size, compact footprint, assembly, systems, materiality, transparency, and mass-customizable frame, it offers a view of a future not so distant.

The variety of ways this house might serve public needs is legion. It can stand alone, or in a row. It can be transparent, opaque, colorless, colorful, fixed, flexible, on a city block, or next to a rural lane. It can be expanded, contracted, altered, adjusted, or simply left alone. As an armature, nothing is better. As space, it is enough, particularly in this age of excess. As the economic crisis subsides and consumers demand economical, innovative products, developers will embrace off-site fabrication. Cellophane House™ and its siblings will have a bright future.

So we built our idea. We planned, we did, we monitored, and we learned from it. We will continue to learn, whether by developing a high-performance scrim for an embassy, or building another house, or designing temporary shelter from a storm. The ideas feed upon one another, informing each with what came before. What is to come after? It may show up again in the zeitgeist. Look for it on a block next to yours.

**Stephen Kieran and James Timberlake**

6.1 Single-family dwelling, suburban site

6.2   Multi-family dwelling, urban site

6.3   Single-family dwelling, exurban site

6.4    Single-family dwelling, waterfront site

# NOTES ON CELLOPHANE

**We know cellophane.**

And, we would be remiss if, diverted by the prototypical schema and largeness of Cellophane House™, we failed to interrogate cellophane itself, both tacitly and technologically.

Cellophane wraps. A seam, edge, or fold—places where the transparent material gathers in layers and crinkles—is made vulnerable by pulling with a fingertip, pen, or knife. Undoing this wrapping—and here you may recall how cellophane sounds—is easy enough; yet unlike paper, where folds may be retraced, cellophane barely exhibits memory. Such lightweight, thin wrappers are not easily refolded; they are slippery, slick, and noisy.

Objects first wrapped and sold in cellophane, and said to be "cellophaned" were luxury items, an affiliation rendered by a relatively high cost per pound. Moisture proofing cellophane, by applying a waxy lacquer coating in a final manufacturing step, propelled cellophane into ubiquity. It first wrapped and moisture proofed cigars and cigarettes; and it later wrapped textiles and preserved bread, meat, and processed foodstuffs. All the while its cost per pound dropped, making possible the wrapping of any object, luxury or commodity, guaranteeing multi-generational cellophane know-how.

Cellophane—lightweight, perfectly transparent, and highly reflective—makes dull objects more interesting. Cellophane transfers its effects, and some mystery, to that which is wrapped. Recall the bit of energy required to recognize objects through cellophane, especially where it has been gathered, cinched, or excessively folded. Here, reflection phenomena abound across multiple surface areas, obscuring the object within. E.I. Du Pont De Nemours & Company, holder of the US rights to cellophane, described it as "the transparent film that sparkles" in the 1950 marketing pamphlet titled *The Story of Cellophane*. Coupled with "moisture proof," cellophane can be described as "moisture proof sparkle"—performance paired with phenomena.

Developer Henry J. Levitt was less interested in performance, and more interested in phenomena (and selling houses), when in 1937 he wrapped an entire neo-colonial house in cellophane. Number 10 Pickwick Road, the model home of his development in Manhasset, New York, was wrapped replete with bow. Levitt seized on cellophane's sparkle, preserving the relationship between object and wrapper, suggesting that the house is nothing without it. In contrast, Cellophane House™ suggests that cellophane is the object.

Yet, we do not know cellophane. It is entirely likely that we have forgotten or have never known what cellophane is.

The first clue is found by dissecting inventor J.E. Brandenberger's made-up name for the material. "Cello" is a contraction of cellulose, and "phane" is a contraction for diaphanous, or lightness, delicacy, and translucency. "Cello" conjoined with "diaphanous," directs us to material origins and material phenomena. Phenomena placed aside momentarily, Cellophane House™ offers a provocation based on cellophane's origins, based on cellulose.

Cellulose, a natural polymer fiber, is plant life's starting structure. It is an abundant natural resource: $1.3 \times 10^9$ megatons of cellulose are produced annually via photosynthesis from water and carbon dioxide. Cellophane can be made from several sources such as wood, cotton, straw, bagasse, or jute. Cotton is the most efficient because its hairs have the highest amount of cellulose content at 90%, the remaining 10% attributed to impurities such as lignin and hemicellulose. On average, trees are 40–

50% cellulose, but several pine species are upwards of 70%. The process that converts cellulose into a transparent coagulated mass, worked out in the late 19th century by Frederick J. Cross and Edward J. Bevan, formed the basic chemistry for creating cellulosics, the first family of synthetic plastics.

Cellophane is "regenerated cellulose," a perplexing term that describes the transformation of cotton gauze or wood pulp into transparent film, a transformation requiring the use of known toxins and pollutants. By steeping the gauze or pulp in lye, and then pressing out the lye, impurities such as lignin and hemi-cellulose are removed, producing pure cellulose in white crumb form which is then exposed to air and aged. Adding carbon disulfide creates a salt of cellulose, a smallish granular yellow crumb, which can be dissolved to become a thick extrudable liquid, or viscose. Dissolution indicates that the opaque to transparent transformation is complete, but the resulting viscose is not yet regenerated cellulose.

The modifier "regenerated" is conjoined to "cellulose" to describe how the dimension of a naturally occurring polymer is chemically manipulated to create cellophane. Cellulose originates as chains varying 5,000 to 10,000 units in length. One closely inspecting the salt of cellulose would consistently find shorter cellulose chains, perhaps on the order of 350 units in length, the carbon disulfide having cut the long polymer chains. Regeneration is simultaneously coupled with cellophane's creation when the viscose, extruded into a film via a slot, comes into contact with a water, salt, and acid bath. This reaction causes the film to gel and cellulose chains to polymerize. Cellulose is put back together—regenerated—as chains 350 units in length reconnect to form longer polymer chains varying 5,000 to 10,000 units in length, the very definition of polymerization. Cellulose is summarily transformed from opaque natural polymer into salt, and from a salt solution into a synthetic polymer film.

Cellophane is a chemically induced moisture proof transparent biodegradable film that sparkles, one originating from opaque renewable resources.

The name Cellophane House™ references a cultural and shared material memory, one recalled via tacit knowledge associated with viewing objects through cellophane and handling cellophane wrappers. By invoking "cellophane" a provocation is made to connect the house to the resources and processes used to achieve lightweight, diaphanous, transparency.

Cellophane House™ is wrapped in a polyethylene terephthalate (PET) membrane, studded with thin-film photovoltaic cells—a film and module composite that prototypes a multi-functional "smart" wrap. PET is a synthetic plastic of various hydrocarbons sourced from petroleum, one that is highly recyclable. As applied to Cellophane House™, PET could be said to be a surrogate material, but not for another high-performing plastic such as ethylene tetrafluoroethylene (ETFE). No, in the presence of the name Cellophane House™, PET may be said to be a surrogate material for "regenerated cellophane," a future transparent plastic film made from renewable resources without adverse affects, one that embodies carbon, and counts biodegradability as an end-of-life option; one that may perform as a multifunctional supra or substrate. And one that gives way to a pellucid architecture. Performance paired with phenomena.

Might we pursue such a material?

**Billie Faircloth**

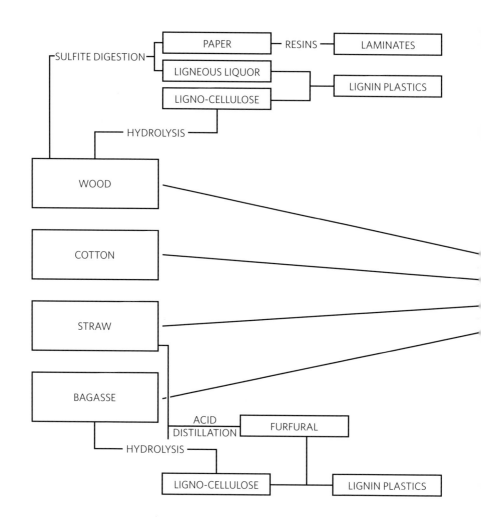

BASED ON GANGLOFF'S ORIGINAL CHART

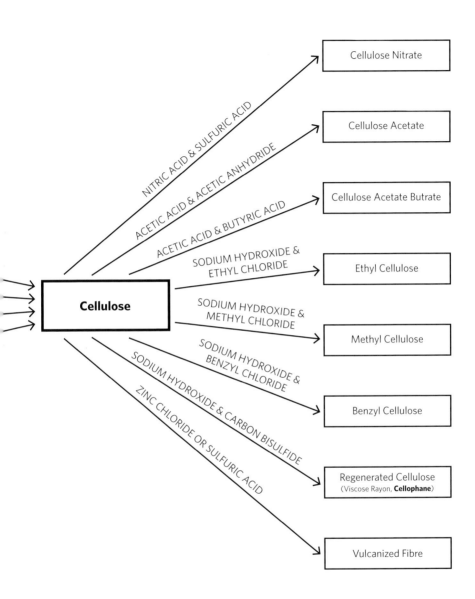

7.1 The Cellulosics, or the family of plastics derived from cellulose,
as diagrammed in the 1945 *Modern Plastics Encyclopedia Issue*.
Bristol, Conn: Plastics Catalogue Corp. 1945. Redrawn.

## KieranTimberlake

Design Partners: Stephen Kieran, James Timberlake

Principal in Charge: David Riz

Project Architect: Steven Johns

Technical Review: Chris Macneal

Project Team: Bradley Baer, Rod Bates, Casey Boss, Derek Brown, Vincent Calabro, Erin Crowe, Peter Curry, Kate Czembor, Mark Davis, Billie Faircloth, David Feaster, Jose Galarza, Alex Gauzza, Laurent Hedquist, David Hincher, Trevor Horst, Elizabeth Kahley, Aaron Knorr, Caleb Knutson, Matthew Krissel, Jeremy Leman, Richard Maimon, Ryan Meillier, Dominic Muren, Jason Niebish, Cesar Querales, Marina Rubina, Sarah Savage, Andrew Schlatter, Paul Worrell

## Consultants

Fabrication and Assembly: Kullman Buildings Corp.

Construction Manager: F.J. Sciame Construction Co., Inc.

On-site Fabricator: Craftweld Fabrication Co., Inc.

On-site Riggers: Budco Enterprises, Inc.

Structural Engineer: CVM Engineers

SmartWrap™ Fabricator: Universal Services Associates, Inc.

Lighting Designer: Arup

Acrylic Stair Fabricator: Capital Plastics Company

**Suppliers**

Structural Frame: Bosch Rexroth Corporation, distributed by Airline Hydraulics Corporation

Floors and Interior Partitions: 3form

Windows and Doors: Schüco USA

LED Lighting: Philips/Color Kinetics

Translucent Roofing: CPI Daylighting Inc.

Acrylic for Stair: Total Plastics Inc.

PET Film: DuPont Teijin Films

Thin Film Technology: PowerFilm, Inc.

Infrared Blocking Film: 3M

Kitchen Casework: Valcucine

Appliances: Miele

Plumbing Fixtures: AF New York

Bathroom Pods: Kullman Buildings Corp. (designed by Hopkins Architects [UK], modified by KieranTimberlake, used with permission from Rice University)

OTHER BOOKS BY KIERANTIMBERLAKE

*Manual: The Architecture of KieranTimberlake*
*refabricating ARCHITECTURE*
*Loblolly House: Elements of a New Architecture*
*KieranTimberlake: Inquiry (Fall 2011)*

CELLOPHANE HOUSE™ is also available as a digital book
For more information visit kierantimberlake.com